D0393986

YA
614.5

Here are some other books
by David Getz you will enjoy:

Frozen Girl
Frozen Man
Life on Mars

PURPLE DEATH

PURPLE DEATH

THE MYSTERIOUS FLU OF 1918

DAVID GETZ

ILLUSTRATIONS BY
PETER McCARTY

Henry Holt and Company ‣ New York

A most appreciative thanks to the following people for speaking with me: Dr. Peter Palese, Dr. Johan Hultin, Kirsty Duncan, Ph.D., Dr. Nancy Cox, Dr. Jeffrey Taubenberger, Dr. Maurice Hilleman, Dr. Dominic Iacuzzio, Dr. Peter Belamarich.

Henry Holt and Company, LLC
Publishers since 1866
115 West 18th Street
New York, New York 10011

Henry Holt and Company is a registered trademark of Henry Holt and Company, LLC

Library of Congress Cataloging-in-Publication Data
Getz, David.
Purple death: the mysterious flu of 1918 / David Getz; illustrations by Peter McCarty.
p.   cm
Includes bibliographical references and index.
Summary: An illustrated overview of the onset, progress, and effects of the flu epidemic
of 1918, which resulted in the deaths of more than half a million people.
1. Influenza—History—20th century—Juvenile literature.   2. Epidemics—History—20th century—
Juvenile literature.   [1. Influenza—History—20th century.   2. Epidemics—History—20th century.
3. Diseases.]   I. McCarty, Peter, ill.   II. Title.
RC150.4 .G48 2000 614.5'18'09041—dc21   00-28134

ISBN 0-8050-5751-X / First Edition—2000
Printed in Mexico
1   3   5   7   9   10   8   6   4   2

As always, for Edy, Max, and Jacqui,
and with great big thanks to Norma Jones,
"the best in the world!"

CONTENTS

In investigations such as we are now pursuing, it should not be so much asked "what has occurred," as "what has occurred that has never occurred before."

—from *Murders in the Rue Morgue,* Edgar Allen Poe

PICNIC

Late in September 1918, a few army officers decided to celebrate. Gathering their wives, they set off for a sunset picnic in the Ohio countryside. The officers were stationed at Camp Sherman, in the town of Chillicothe, where they were training young men to become soldiers. There was a terrible war in Europe, and once these soldiers were ready, they would be sent to France to fight the Germans. As the officers knew well, many of the young men would be killed soon after they reached Europe. Some could expect to have their legs blown off by land mines. Some could expect to be blinded by poisonous gas. A few would be driven mad by the noise, the confusion, the stench, and the horrors of war.

So what was there to celebrate?

Camp Sherman, they believed, had escaped the worst of the flu. At a time when the flu was killing thousands of people, the camp suffered relatively few deaths, and that was cause for celebration. There was something deadly and mysterious about the flu of 1918.

"One of the odd features of this influenza virus was that it selectively killed young healthy adults," explains Dr. Jeffrey Taubenberger, a scientist who is trying to learn more about the 1918 flu. Normally influenza—flu— viruses are only a threat to the lives of babies, very old people, and those who are already ill. "Young adults and children tend to get over the flu," Dr. Taubenberger explains. "They get it, but they don't tend to die. But in this case, the people who were most likely to die of the flu were twenty- to forty-year-olds."

Camp Sherman had a population of more than 30,000 people, most of them twenty to forty years old. The flu spread easily through the air. Even before he knew he was sick, a person who was infected could cough, sneeze, or breathe out millions of flu virus particles into the air.

In a crowded area, like an army barracks, one infected soldier could spread the flu to hundreds of others in minutes.

Other military camps had been hit hard by the flu, their hospitals overrun by its victims, their morgues filled. Camp Sherman had been lucky, and the officers on their way to the picnic felt grateful. But only three days later, the flu virus hit the camp with a terrible force. One soldier after another began shuffling up to the camp hospital. They ran high fevers. Everything hurt. They felt as if they had been beaten and battered. They were desperately weak and no longer able to stand.

The blood vessels surrounding their lungs began to leak, filling the air passages with blood. Many were frantically short of breath. Their faces were blotchy, their skin turning purple from lack of oxygen. They were drowning in their own body fluids. Delirious from lack of oxygen, these young men rolled and thrashed about on their beds and cots, moaning, mumbling, and spitting up blood.

The hospital quickly ran out of space and supplies to care for the sick. New, temporary hospitals were set up in barracks and officers' quarters. Unable to avoid the disease, doctors and nurses caught it. Within weeks, there weren't enough medical personnel to care for the growing number of desperately ill young men. In the next three months, the flu struck nearly 8,000 people at Camp Sherman, killing more than a thousand of them. On one day alone, it claimed about 125 of its victims, many of them boys who had left home only weeks before.

Parents were desperate to see their young sons. They flocked to the camp. They pleaded with the doctors to do more. They slept in hallways. They begged to be allowed to take their children back home.

In 1918, there was little anybody could do. There were no medicines and no medical treatments that could stop what many soldiers had begun calling the Purple Death. Still, people from surrounding towns sent telegrams with advice. Some suggested placing shotguns under the beds of the ill because the barrels would suck out the fever. Others urged doctors to apply poultices (warm, wet patches of fabric) to the chests of the stricken. The telegrams suggested filling the poultices with spinach, flax seed, onions, turnips, asparagus, and even kerosene. But the doctors knew the truth: there was no defense against this killer.

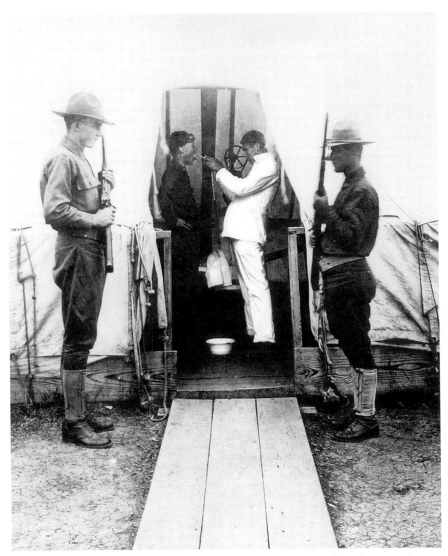

An army doctor sprays a soldier's throat to try to prevent him from getting the flu. *Courtesy of the National Museum of Health and Medicine, Armed Forces Institute of Pathology.*

Within weeks there were so many dead that there was no place to keep the bodies. Officers took over a local theater and turned its stage into a morgue. They lined up the dead in long rows and waited daily for coffins to arrive. Often, the bodies could not be identified. Before killing them, the flu caused high fevers and created a lack of oxygen that made its victims wild and irrational. Confused and frantic soldiers often ripped off their own dog tags, the metal identification tags that they wore on chains around their necks. Officers were given lists to try and identify the dead, but sometimes they could only guess.

By October 12, the flu had run its course at Camp Sherman. No new cases were reported to the hospital, though many soldiers continued to die from the flu or its complications. Slowly, Camp Sherman returned to its mission, sending young men to war.

What had happened to the common flu? How had it become so lethal?

WAR FEVER

The flu that struck Camp Sherman was not a new disease. Influenza has been around for hundreds if not thousands of years. It is a seasonal illness that tends to infect people in late winter every year. In the early fourteenth century, Italian scientists began calling it "influenza," or the "influence," because they believed that when the planets appeared a certain way in the night sky, they could influence a person's body to suddenly run a high fever and develop muscle aches, a sore throat, coughing, and fatigue. At about the same time, German scholars observed the illness and said it was caused by eating too many sour apples and salted fish.

Flu pandemics were not new to the world in 1918,

either. An "epidemic" is a disease that is widespread throughout a given area. A "pandemic" is a disease that quickly spreads through populations and crosses over borders to infect thousands, even millions of people. In 1580, a disease that was probably the flu began in Asia and quickly spread through Europe, Africa, and America, nearly wiping out entire villages in Spain and Italy. Similar outbreaks have occurred a few times every century since then, though none has been so devastating as the 1918 flu pandemic.

On April 6, 1917, the United States entered World War I by declaring war on Germany. The war had been dragging on in Europe for three years, killing many young soldiers, as well as bringing widespread famine and disease. President Woodrow Wilson hoped that U.S. soldiers could bring the war to an end. Quickly, America became a war machine. Every aspect of life was supposed to contribute to the war effort. Movie actors led parades down major streets to raise money for weapons. Newspapers urged mothers to knit warm scarves to send to the young American soldiers in Europe. Teachers urged their students to save peach pits, which would be burned into the charcoal that was used as gas-mask filters by the soldiers in Europe. And on June 4, 1917, nearly 10 million young American men signed up to become soldiers.

By early 1918, army training camps, each of them overcrowded with tens of thousands of recruits, dotted the American countryside. From these camps, young men were stuffed into trains, shuffled off to other camps,

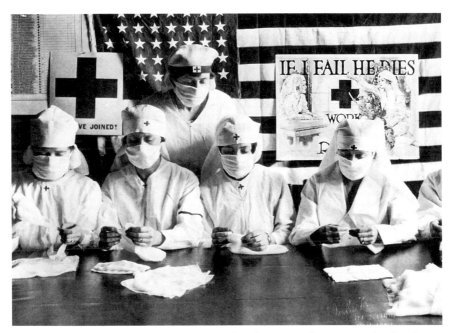

Red Cross volunteers made thousands of gauze influenza masks for the "boys" fighting in the war. *Courtesy of the American Red Cross.*

and then placed onto ships, which steamed them away to the bustling ports of Europe. The flu travels best in crowded conditions. America in 1918 was the perfect staging ground for a pandemic.

It began sometime in the spring, somewhere in the Midwest. The first reported case of the flu was at Camp Funston, Kansas, on March 4, 1918. From its outbreak in Funston, the flu traveled in the noses, throats, and lungs of soldiers to other military bases throughout the country. At this point, the flu was not yet the horrible killer it would become, though it did seem to single out young men to attack with exceptional violence. "It really wasn't that bad in the spring," says Dr. Taubenberger. "It was worse than your normal flu, but not so much that people took notice at the time."

By April, the flu was infecting civilians as well as soldiers throughout the country. Scientists refer to this time period of the 1918 flu as its "first wave." This first wave washed up on the shores of Europe in early April, as American troopships docked in France and unloaded infected American soldiers. The virus quickly spread through the already hungry and ill civilians and soldiers

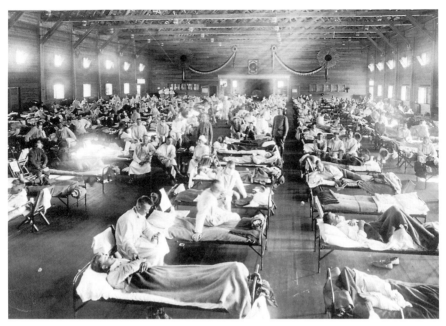

An emergency hospital had to be set up in Camp Funston, Kansas, to accommodate all the flu patients. *Courtesy of the National Museum of Health and Medicine, Armed Forces Institute of Pathology.*

of war-torn France. In May, it hit Portugal and Spain. In Spain, the flu became a news story. For the first time, people reading about this new disease started calling it the Spanish flu. Within three months, the first wave had washed over the world. Yet the flu was still not the killer it would become.

Then on August 22, American soldiers began reporting to the local hospital in Brest, France, with lung failure.

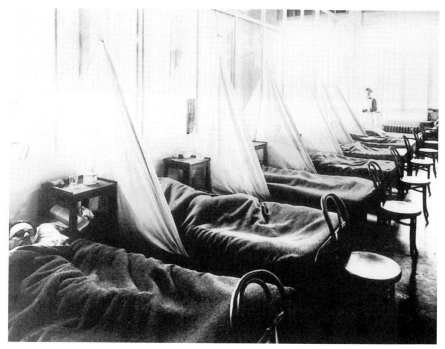

The influenza ward of an army hospital in Aix-les-Bains, France. *Courtesy of the National Museum of Health and Medicine, Armed Forces Institute of Pathology.*

Only hours after showing the symptoms of the flu, soldiers were suddenly turning blue and dying. Something inexplicable had happened to the flu in France. The "second wave" had begun.

Brest was a major port city in France and the landing site for American soldiers entering the war. It was the perfect place for the flu to begin its second assault on the world. Within days, ships carrying infected passengers with this new, more virulent flu docked at Boston, Massachusetts, and Freetown, Sierra Leone, in Africa. From these three ports the flu spread out to infect nearly every village, town, and city in the world. It traveled by boat to such remote places as Iceland, Samoa, Alaska, and New Zealand. Trains carried it through India and Africa. Prisoners of war pushed it across European borders as they returned home. Refugees fleeing war and famine also helped spread the disease from one country to another.

When the flu returned to the United States, it began to shut down town after town, overwhelming entire cities with fear, confusion, and helplessness.

EVEN THE CIRCUS STOPPED TOURING

The disease first struck Nashville, Tennessee, in late September. It began its attack in Nashville's southern section, where workers for a nearby gunpowder plant lived in crowded conditions. Infected workers carried the disease east. The disease spread like a stain through the fabric of Nashville, infecting more than 40,000 people from the first of October to the middle of November. More than 15,000 would die.

The disease hit the city at a particularly bad time. Nearly a third of Nashville's doctors were away in Europe treating wounded and sick soldiers. That left only 250 doctors to treat its 40,000 sick patients, one doctor for every 160 people. And that was if the doctors stayed healthy, which they didn't. Many caught the disease and a few died. Nurses quickly became Nashville's guardians and protectors. They had to find patients, then determine how sick they were and what treatment they needed. When Nashville's hospitals became overcrowded, nurses treated patients at home. This turned out to be a good thing. Patients who were admitted to a hospital increased their chances of catching bacterial pneumonia from other patients. Today, bacterial pneumonia is a disease that can be treated with antibiotics. In 1918, before antibiotics were discovered, bacterial pneumonia killed half of its victims. Public health officials in Nashville soon recognized some ugly facts: there was no cure for the flu, and there was no cure for bacterial pneumonia.

How could they save the people of their city?

If they could not cure the flu, then the next best thing was to prevent people from getting it. On October 8, Nashville officials outlawed all public gatherings. They closed theaters, carnivals, dance halls, pool parlors, and movie houses. Officials thought that although they couldn't cure a person once he or she caught the flu, maybe they could prevent that person from spreading the

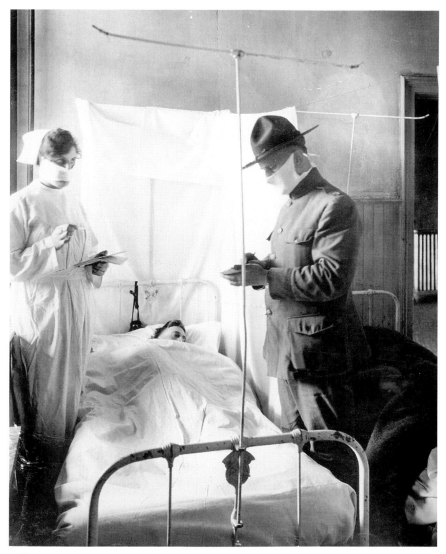

In some army hospitals, beds were placed head to foot so flu patients did not breathe directly into the faces of the men next to them. *Courtesy of the American Red Cross.*

disease in crowds. Ministers were ordered to stop holding church services. Frightened parents refused to send their children to school. Dr. E. L. Bishop, a doctor working for the Nashville Board of Health, informed everyone that the flu was spread by laughing, coughing, and sneezing, and that the people of Nashville should refrain from "kissing, and especially the nonessential variety."

It didn't work. The flu continued to ravage Nashville.

Suffering and death followed the flu pandemic to every town and city.

On October 16, Dr. Royal Copeland, director of New York City's Department of Health, cited that in the previous twenty-four hours, 4,925 new cases of the flu had been reported in the city, with 479 cases of pneumonia and 200 flu-related deaths. Desperate for people to help care for the sick, Dr. Copeland "appealed to persons having more than one servant to assign one to the Health Department to work under orders." The servants, he promised, "would be well paid and their health guarded."

In Philadelphia, the flu and pneumonia killed 700 people in the first week of October; 2,600 the second week; and 4,500 the third. Countless thousands were ill. There were too few doctors. The shortage of nurses was so severe that a Philadelphia hospital advertised for "any person with two hands willing to work." During the first week of October, nearly 500 policemen called in sick. The fire department and the sanitation department were hit just as badly.

The Red Cross Motor Corps helps transport flu victims in St. Louis, Missouri. *Courtesy of the American Red Cross.*

"About a third of the U.S. population was infected with it," Dr. Taubenberger says. "There was a massive shortage of medical care of all kinds. And then there were all the macabre things that went along. There was a massive shortage of grave diggers and undertakers, coffins and coffin makers."

In Camden, New Jersey, just across the Delaware River from Philadelphia, people died so quickly that town officials forced convicts to dig graves under the watch of armed guards. Cemetery administrators could no longer keep accurate records of where the dead were buried. Graves were mismarked, and relatives could not find where their loved ones had been laid to rest.

Health officials and public leaders were desperate. They tried everything they could to slow down the disease, to limit the number of people it infected. In Chicago, police were instructed to arrest anybody who sneezed or coughed in public.

In Hartford, Connecticut, teachers were told to immediately send home any student who showed any signs of a cold or the flu. They were also instructed to tell these students to "go to bed immediately and not wait until

A public service notice in a trolley car in Cincinnati, Ohio. *Courtesy of the American Red Cross.*

tomorrow. Take a laxative. Drink much plain water. Have plenty of fresh air in the room. Send for a doctor and stay in bed at least forty-eight hours after the symptoms have subsided."

San Francisco's leaders passed a law that required everyone to wear masks when outside. The masks, which were to be worn over the nose and mouth, were made of four layers of gauze.

The governor of Alaska ordered that each town and village be surrounded by a line of red flags. Strangers were not allowed to cross that line. The governor ordered cabins to be built outside of towns and furnished with food and necessities for traveling trappers and fishermen. Some villagers sent armed guards miles south of their towns to turn back anyone who might be carrying the flu.

Around the world, cities shut down. As in Nashville, public health officials banned public gatherings. One town after another ordered the closing of movie houses, theaters, and saloons. Some public health officials banned Sunday church services and asked religious leaders to refrain from holding funerals. Leaders either shut schools, or parents refused to send their children, fearing for their lives. Sylvia Diamond, a survivor of the epidemic, remembers, "My mother just kept me home in my backyard. I wasn't allowed to go anywhere."

Phone companies urged people to make only essential

calls. There were not enough operators to make the connections. Police, fire, and sanitation departments lost too many workers to be effective. Small businesses temporarily closed. That fall, even the circus stopped touring.

It was the deadliest six months in history. The flu infected nearly 2 billion people, just about everybody on the planet. Nobody knows just how many people it killed, though scientists estimate that 20 to 40 million people died from the flu or its complications. In some places like Alaska, Samoa, and New Zealand, entire towns were nearly wiped out in a matter of days. In October alone, the flu killed more people than HIV did in its first ten years.

Then, sometime in the late spring of 1919—before anyone knew what was causing this flu—the virus started to disappear. Whatever had caused the pandemic was vanishing. Scientists urgently needed to track it down. They had some very important questions that needed to be answered.

What had made this flu so deadly? Could it return?

The hunt was on.

THE HUNT BEGINS

The hunt for answers began almost immediately. In 1918, scientists knew that all communicable diseases (illnesses that can be passed from one person to another) were caused by microbes, tiny one-celled life forms that were only visible under the microscope. They also knew that each communicable disease was caused by only one specific microbe. What was the microbe that caused the deadly flu?

Scientists in 1918 were like the police in a town that had been hit by a series of mysterious fires. Until they caught the culprit who had set the blazes, they could not promise the people that they would be safe.

The United States Navy began a hunt in November

1918 at a training station on Deer Island in Massachusetts. It started by persuading sixty-eight sailors who were in jail for a variety of crimes to volunteer to risk their lives. The navy promised these sailors their freedom if they allowed themselves to be experimented on. The navy wanted to know where the flu microbe hid as it was transmitted from one person to another. In one series of experiments, they injected some of these sailors with the blood or phlegm of flu victims. In other experiments, they asked the volunteers to shake hands with flu patients or place their faces near flu patients who spoke or coughed.

The navy failed to find out where the mysterious flu microbe hid. None of the test subjects fell ill with the flu. The navy then tried a similar experiment in San Francisco. Scientists convinced fifty sailors from the naval training base to have the secretions of flu patients placed into their own bodies. Again, nobody developed the flu. Amazingly, as the disease was rampaging through the military like a man swinging a bat in a crowd, none of the navy's subjects fell ill with the flu.

Scientists examined the respiratory tracts of flu victims

to see if there were any suspicious bacteria that could have caused the disease. There were plenty. Some of these bacteria were connected to diseases like pneumonia and strep throat. Scientists found other bacteria that were more mysterious. Could any of them have caused the flu?

Each bacteria was tested. Each failed to produce the flu in healthy people. It seemed that the microbes present in the throats and lungs of flu victims arrived after the flu had already begun its assault. These bacteria were like looters following an initial break-in. Unsettling questions began to arise in the minds of some scientists. What if the microbe that caused the flu left before the patient died? What if it quickly did its damage, then escaped and was no longer present at the time of autopsy? Or what if the flu was caused by a virus, a disease-causing agent that was too small to be seen with the microscopes that were available in 1918?

Flu microbe hunters needed to complete a series of steps to prove they had found the cause of the disease. First, they had to find and isolate the same microbe at the site of every flu infection. Secondly, they had to grow that microbe in the laboratory, outside the bodies of flu patients. Thirdly, they had to then show that their suspect microbe was capable of causing the flu in healthy people. Finally, scientists had to be able to retrieve their suspicious microbe from the bodies of the people they had just made sick.

It was not until the 1930s, however, that scientists began to complete most of these steps. In the winter of 1933, England had an epidemic of a relatively mild flu. Three scientists, Wilson Smith, C. H. Andrewes, and P. P. Laidlaw, suspected a virus was responsible. Though they didn't know much about viruses, they did know that viruses are much smaller than bacteria and capable of causing disease. To test their theory, they took mucus from the throats of people who had just started to complain of having a flu and passed that mucus through filters with holes so tiny that even one-celled bacteria couldn't go through. They took the filtered fluid, which was now free from bacteria, and placed it in the noses of a variety of healthy animals in their labs. None of the animals got sick.

Then they tried the fluid in the noses of ferrets. It was as if they had turned on a switch. The ferrets' noses began to

run. The ferrets acted weak and achy. They ran high fevers. The ferrets had got the flu! But a ferret is not a human. Could this still invisible virus make a healthy human sick?

A few years later, researchers got their answer. As time passed, one flu-stricken ferret passed on its infection to another until, in 1936, the 196th flu-sick ferret sneezed on one of the British scientists, C. H. Stuart Harris. Two days later, Stuart Harris had the flu.

Smith, Laidlaw, and Andrewes had discovered the hiding place of the flu microbe. They had isolated their suspicious microbe in the respiratory secretions of recently sick flu patients. They had used their microbe to make healthy individuals sick with the flu. True, they could not actually see their microbe, nor could they grow it in a culture outside of the body of an infected individual. Still, this was a major achievement. For the first time, scientists had proven that the flu was caused by a virus.

But this was the 1933 flu virus, a mild strain. Where was the 1918 strain? Why was it so lethal, while the 1933 strain was not? To begin to solve these riddles, scientists first had to ask themselves a bigger question: what is a virus?

STOP WHAT YOU ARE DOING! MAKE MORE OF ME!

A virus is different from every other life-form on earth. To begin with, they are strange-looking and incredibly small. The flu virus, for example, is round and has a halo of spikes. Millions, if not billions, of flu viruses can fit into a single cell, and a single cell can be smaller than the period at the end of this sentence. Scientists could not even see viruses until the invention of the electron microscope in the 1930s.

Viruses are the only life-form we know of that does not eat, drink, breathe, or produce waste. Viruses cannot reproduce or travel by themselves. They must be forcibly sent from one victim to another. So how does a virus enter your body and harm you?

The flu virus travels in droplets of mucus that come from the throats and noses of infected people. A person sick with the flu can eject thousands of flu particles up to twenty-five feet into the air in a single sneeze. The air around a flu victim becomes an invisible, contaminated cloud. Once you accidentally step into this cloud and inhale, you bring the virus into your body.

Each type of virus targets one specific kind of cell in its victims. Some viruses attack nerve cells, while others attack skin, muscle, or bone cells. Flu viruses prefer epithelial cells, which line your respiratory tract. As you inhale infected air, thousands of flu particles brush against these epithelial cells.

"It is not a very efficient process," says flu expert Dr. Peter Palese, the chairman of the Department of Microbiology at the Mount Sinai School of Medicine in New York. "There may be a hundred particles coming in, but only one really succeeds in getting into a cell. It's not a one-to-one shot. Most will not make it."

Once the flu virus attaches to an epithelial cell, which is thousands of times bigger, the epithelial cell draws it inside. Like all viruses, the flu virus is little more than a package of instructions on how to make more of itself. Beneath its spiky coating are eight strings of molecules (long chains of chemicals) called RNA. That's short for ribonucleic acid, which provides information to the cell it invades. After the flu virus enters an epithelial cell, it injects its RNA into the cell's nucleus. In the nucleus the flu's RNA tells the cell, "Stop what you are doing! Make more of me!" The epithelial cell has no choice. Its nucleus follows these new directions and becomes a factory for the production of more flu viruses.

Eventually, these new viral particles burst out through the cell wall to infect neighboring epithelial cells. It's at this point that you begin to feel sick. But it's not really the viral invasion that makes you feel "fluish"—your symptoms are mostly due to your body's response to this invasion. Inflammation at the site of the infections gives you a sore throat. You cough and sneeze to expel the invaders. As your epithelial cells are destroyed, they release certain chemicals that travel through your bloodstream and cause your muscles to hurt. Your body releases other chemicals that cause your body temperature to rise. While this fever makes you feel terrible, it helps destroy

the viral particles. Fever also increases blood flow, bringing your body's defenses to the site of battle. If all goes well, you only miss a few days of school.

Yet, in 1918, millions of healthy young people died from the flu. Somehow that flu was different from others, but how?

The only way to answer that question is to find the 1918 flu.

ALASKA

In 1951, a group of scientists went to Alaska to dig up the bodies of the dead. Perhaps there, within the lungs of the flu's Arctic victims, they would find the virus preserved and frozen. They wanted to bring it back to their labs in Iowa to study and, hopefully, develop a cure or prevention, should this deadly flu ever return.

One of the scientists, Johan Hultin, recalls how the project began. He was a graduate student from Sweden who had come to Iowa to study microbiology. He heard a lecture about the 1918 flu and learned that while scientists suspected quite a bit about the flu, they actually knew very little. The lecturer explained that to learn more, scientists needed to discover where the 1918 virus was hiding and bring it back. He suggested that it might be frozen in the lungs of people who had been buried in permanently frozen ground, or permafrost. He advised looking in the northern parts of the world, such as Alaska, Russia, and Scandinavia.

After the lecture, Hultin approached his advisor, Albert McKee, and asked for permission to search for flu victims in Alaska as part of his studies. McKee agreed.

Hultin knew some things about Alaska. In 1949, he had worked as a paleontologist's helper in Alaska, looking for fossilized bones of ancient horses. His supervisor was the paleontologist Otto Geist. Perhaps Geist could help him track down the burial grounds of flu victims.

Hultin contacted Geist, who put him in touch with missionaries, who sent him church records of Alaskan burials in 1918. The records listed who had died, what they had died from, how quickly they had died after becoming ill, and where they were buried. After months of research, Hultin came up with three suitable locations.

"So I got some funding," he recalls. "I went to the three sites in Alaska, dug into the graves with permission from the Eskimos, and found one of the sites very adequate. It

was the Teller Mission, on the Seward Peninsula. The bodies were frozen. The site looked great."

McKee, along with Jack Layton, a pathologist, a scientist who studies the causes and effects of diseases, joined Hultin in Anchorage. Here the team confronted its first problem. They had planned to preserve the tissue samples from the graves with frozen carbon dioxide, or "dry ice."

"But we had so many delays, our dry ice evaporated," Hultin says. "The whole expedition was about to fall apart because we couldn't find dry ice. Sitting in Anchorage, we talked about this, and suddenly it came to me. Dry ice! Dry ice! That's the white powdery stuff in fire extinguishers!"

Quickly, the team hired taxis and set off to buy all the fire extinguishers they could find in Anchorage. Then they left for Nome. As their plane carried them aloft, the scientists aboard considered the consequences of a mistake. What if one of them accidentally became infected with the 1918 virus? There were still no weapons to fight the flu. What if the virus somehow escaped back into the world? Could they be responsible for a new pandemic?

The virus had been merciless to the Eskimos living in

remote Alaskan outposts. In one week, the flu killed 72 of the 80 villagers who lived in Teller. Soldiers from a nearby fort had to be brought in to break through the frozen ground in order to bury the dead. The bodies were lined up in long mass graves with a cross at each end. These nineteen graves were dug six feet deep, three feet below the frost line. The soil above the frost line thawed every summer. A body buried above this line would float up to the surface as the ground melted. The soil below the frost line usually stayed frozen throughout the year. This deeper soil is the permafrost, and it was the safest place to bury the Eskimos who had died from this contagious disease. There was no chance of the flu virus, if it remained in their lungs, escaping back up to the surface—unless, of course, somebody dug them up.

Which is what Geist, Layton, Hultin, and McKee planned to do. A bush pilot flew them from Nome to the inlet where the Teller Mission was located. The plane landed opposite the mission, and the team then took a whaling boat made from walrus hides across the inlet. Carrying their autopsy equipment and fire extinguishers on their backs, they trudged about four miles across soft, soggy tundra to the site of the graves.

What would they uncover?

While the cause of the 1918 flu had remained undiscovered, researchers had begun to learn more about the common flu. They knew that it was a virus, and that it could change from year to year. They had also begun to learn about immunology, the study of how bodies defend themselves against disease. Hultin's team hoped to use this new knowledge of immunology to create a vaccine that could prevent people from catching the 1918 flu if it ever came back.

For the scientists from Iowa to be able to create their vaccine against the 1918 flu, they would first need to recover some virus particles. Then they would have to bring these particles back to their lab and somehow revive them. Even if it were possible to revive the 1918 flu virus, it might be dangerous to do so.

Even so, the team began digging on June 25. Outsiders were not allowed near the site for fear they could possibly catch a reawakened flu.

The Iowa team of researchers digging in Alaska in 1951. *Courtesy of Dr. Johan Hultin.*

"We told the local people that this was dangerous stuff we were doing," Hultin recalls. "So nobody showed up. We wore masks to protect ourselves, though we now know that masks are useless against influenza."

Wearing surgical gloves and using sterilized instruments, the scientists began their operation. They cut samples from the lungs, kidneys, spleens, and brains of their subjects. They placed these samples in thermal jugs, spraying the jugs with the fire extinguishers to make sure they stayed frozen.

It was at about this time that a violent storm hit, raising dangerous waves in the bay. Returning by whaling boat to their plane was no longer possible. Calling upon local Eskimos for help, the scientists were able to trek over land and eventually make their way back to their small plane. After twenty-four hours of digging, surgery, and Arctic travel, they left for Iowa.

"Every time we had a landing, Seattle, Anchorage, or in between, I squirted more frozen carbon dioxide ice into those thermal jugs. It made a huge noise," Hultin remembers. "But that saved it. When we arrived in Iowa, the samples were still frozen."

In Iowa, the team tried to culture the virus in fertilized chicken eggs. This is the technique that is still used to grow flu virus to be used for vaccines. A microscopic quantity of flu is injected into the air sac in the egg just above the yolk and developing baby chicken. After a few days, the egg produces enough new virus to fill a tablespoon. When this occurs, the top of the egg is removed and the virus is extracted.

HOW VACCINES WORK

Immunology is the study of how the body defends itself. When a flu virus invades the respiratory tract, the body fights back in a number of ways. Antibodies are microscopically small proteins that latch on to viruses to prevent them from entering a cell. Antibodies also act as flags, marking viruses so that other parts of the immune system can destroy them. Each virus causes the body to produce a specific matching antibody. The flu virus of 1918 caused the body to produce different antibodies than the flu virus of 1928 or 1938 did. Antibodies can be used by scientists to determine the identity of a virus that has attacked a person, just as fingerprints are used to determine the identity of a criminal. Interestingly, the one thing scientists had learned about the 1918 flu was that its victims had the same flu antibodies that pigs had to a swine flu.

Antibodies serve another function besides identification. Even after a virus has left your body, the antibodies to that virus stay in your bloodstream and continue to roam through your body like armed guards, making you immune to a second attack. If you are once more exposed to that identical virus, the antibodies to it will multiply and render it harmless before it can make you seriously ill again.

You can be made immune to a virus with a "vaccine," an injection of either dead or weakened virus. Your immune system recognizes the virus and responds by thinking it's under attack. It immediately begins producing the appropriate antibodies to fight what it thinks is an infection. Even though no infection comes, the antibodies remain, keeping you immune to that particular virus should it ever arrive.

If you were to be injected with a flu vaccine this year, it would cause you to create antibodies that would make you immune to this year's flu only. Each year the flu changes, usually just enough so that the antibodies you have to one year's strain will not be as effective against the following year's strain. This sort of change is called "drift." Sometimes, something unusual happens to the flu virus and it changes so much, so strangely, that the antibodies you have from previous years are completely useless against it. This large change is called "shift." Today, scientists think that when the flu shifts, it becomes capable of creating a pandemic.

The team in Iowa tried to grow the virus they had retrieved in eggs, but they had no luck. They even tried injecting a liquid mixture of their samples into ferrets, a dangerous experiment, since, if they did develop the flu, the animals could cough and sneeze and give the disease right back to the scientists. The pandemic could have started all over again, but it didn't. The team tried every possible way to grow the flu virus from their tissue samples, but they failed. The flu was still hiding, and the questions were still unanswered. Could the deadly flu come back?

In 1976, public health officials thought it did.

THE DEATH OF PRIVATE DAVID LEWIS

For those with any sense of history, the news in February 1976 was frightening. Private David Lewis, an army recruit at Fort Dix, New Jersey, was dead. Sick with typical flu symptoms, Lewis had ignored his doctor's orders to stay in the barracks for two days and get some sleep. Instead he joined his fellow recruits for a grueling five-mile hike and training session in the early February snow. He collapsed on the march back. Army medical personnel rushed Lewis to the hospital. They were too late. Doctors declared him dead on arrival.

This was 1976; young healthy men were not supposed to die from the flu anymore. That had only happened in 1918. Had the mysterious flu returned?

Lewis had been only one of many recruits complaining of flu symptoms. That in itself was not unusual for a crowded military camp in winter. Many recruits returning to the base from their homes had brought the flu with them, spreading it easily in their crowded housing situation. Hundreds of the recruits were even sick enough to require hospitalization. Wondering what virus had hit their camp, the army medical personnel had sent throat swabbings from nineteen of the patients to the New Jersey Public Health Department for identification.

Researchers testing the samples found that eleven of the recruits were suffering from nothing more unusual than that year's flu, which was called the A/Victoria strain. But what about those other eight? Something was strange. The New Jersey scientists could not identify the virus making these people sick. Samples of their throat swabbings were sent to the Centers for Disease Control in Atlanta, Georgia. On February 4, the same day these samples arrived, David Lewis collapsed and died. A throat washing from Lewis was quickly sent down to the CDC to be analyzed as well. On February 12, the CDC made an unsettling discovery. Three of the recruits, along with Davis, showed antibodies to a swine flu.

In 1976, many researchers believed that after the 1918 virus passed through the human population, it changed, then settled back into the pig population. The 1918 flu became solely a swine flu. From 1918 to 1976, scientists believed that while pigs could spread the swine flu among themselves, and on rare occasion could pass it on to a human, it could no longer be spread from one person to another. That strain of the swine flu had disappeared in 1919.

Did the few cases of swine flu at Fort Dix indicate that the swine flu had changed back into a human flu? Was Private Lewis the first victim? Was the 1918 pandemic about to return? Scientists were not sure. They ruled out the possibility that each recruit caught the disease directly from a pig. The soldiers caught it from each other. But perhaps this was just an odd exception. Could the crowded, physically stressful living conditions of the recruits have contributed to this unusual event? Would this new swine flu outbreak virus soon burn itself out like a single match?

Many health experts were worried about the possibility of a pandemic. The surface of the flu virus particle itself was significantly different from the A/Victoria strain then circulating throughout the world. This change was a shift. The last two times the virus had shifted, flu pandemics had occurred, first in 1957, then in 1968. Though both were much less severe than the 1918 pandemic, each killed tens of thousands of people.

There were different theories about when pandemics could be expected. Some scientists thought that this new shift might lead to a new pandemic. Others suspected that the flu pandemics followed some sort of eleven-year cycle, and that a new pandemic was due soon. Medical historians noted that the 1918 pandemic began with separate, isolated outbreaks before the flu exploded worldwide. The epidemic at Fort Dix might be the first isolated outbreak of another flu pandemic.

The prospect was terrifying. In 1918, approximately 20 million Americans came down with the virus, and about half a million of them died in a little more than six months. In 1976, the United States was twice as crowded, and jet travel made the spread of the disease much quicker. It would be easy for flu victims not yet showing signs of the disease to board planes for Los Angeles, Chicago, Texas, or New York and infect all the other passengers during their flights. What took weeks or months in 1918 could now take only hours.

There was still no cure for the flu, but there was immunization. Scientists could prevent people from getting the flu, or at least from getting a bad case of it. The whole process of identifying, making a vaccine, and testing it takes about six months. Before the swine flu appeared, the government had recommended that drug companies produce 40 million doses of A/Victoria vaccine. This was just enough to immunize the people to whom the flu was ordinarily a threat: the elderly and those with respiratory ailments. But if this was the 1918 plague, then all 200 million Americans were in danger.

Was it even possible to make that much vaccine? Where would the eggs come from? And if it was possible, could the vaccine be made, tested, sent out to clinics and doctors around the country, and injected into the arms of all Americans faster than the flu could spread?

The past was not reassuring. In 1957, the Asian flu, a

pandemic strain, was reported in China six months before it hit the United States. In 1968, America had five months' warning that a flu was coming. Yet in both cases, the government and drug companies failed to immunize enough people in time to prevent tens of thousands from dying from the flu.

Scientists and health advisors met in Washington to decide what to do. Some thought that everyone should just wait to see if the swine flu turned into a pandemic. Perhaps, they reasoned, vaccines should be produced but kept in warehouses and only taken out in case of a pandemic. Other scientists were less cautious. They argued that if a pandemic was coming, there was no time to wait. Vaccines had to be produced immediately, and people had to be inoculated.

On March 24, 1976, President Gerald Ford announced that he would request Congress to raise $135 million to help pay for the inoculation of "every man, woman, and child in the United States."

What followed could have ended in disaster.

First, it was nearly impossible to make enough vaccine. Then, the vaccine that was made was not effective in children. They had to be inoculated twice. Finally, the inoculation program was hopelessly slow. It was supposed to start in June, well before school started in September and children began spending time in crowded classrooms with poor ventilation, the perfect environment for the flu virus to spread. In 1957, the flu pandemic began as schools opened in the fall. Yet inoculation didn't begin until October and then only a small fraction of Americans received their shots, not nearly enough to stop a pandemic from spreading.

Thankfully, the flu pandemic never came. The swine flu of Fort Dix simply disappeared, probably slipping back into the pig population. America was safe—and lucky.

THE LONGEST WALK
OF HER LIFE

Dr. Kirsty Duncan wanted to save lives. "Around 1993, I became very interested in the Spanish flu," she says. "I was horrified that we didn't know what caused it." She was aware of the failed Iowa expedition more than forty years earlier. She was also aware of a top secret army mission to Alaska, called Project George, led by Dr. Maurice Hilleman in the 1950s.

That mission, like the one from Iowa, set out to find and recover the virus from frozen bodies. The army had a good reason for hunting down the 1918 virus: it had killed 43,000 of its soldiers in just a few months. Of the American soldiers who died during World War I, 85 out of every 100 were killed not in battle but in their beds by the flu. Decades later, the U.S. military, with all its atomic weapons, planes, and bombs, was still completely defenseless against the virus should it return. Though details about Project George are still top secret, Dr. Duncan knew that it was a complete failure.

She refused to give up. "I had a background in geography and anthropology," Dr. Duncan explains, "and I figured if I could find bodies of people who had died of the Spanish flu and were buried in permafrost, the bodies might be preserved, along with the virus that killed them."

So she began searching for accounts of bodies buried in permafrost. She read through the death certificates of more than a thousand Alaskans. Were there any other bodies buried in the permafrost that could still harbor the flu? None seemed promising. She thought of Russia, where the flu had hit hard, and where the north was covered in frozen ground. The Russian government was not helpful. Then she spoke to a friend returning from Svalbard, Norway.

A chain of islands, Svalbard is about 600 miles from the North Pole. Nearly two thirds of it is permanently covered in glaciers.

"He had just led an expedition across a glacier," Dr. Duncan says. "And he mentioned the permafrost. I got excited. I knew the disease had been in Norway. I guessed if people went up to Svalbard to work in the mines—there were coal mines up there—they could have gotten the disease."

Could they have been buried beneath the permafrost?

Dr. Duncan began her inquiry. She contacted the Norwegian authorities, who told her she had a hard time ahead. There were no government records because Svalbard didn't become part of Norway until 1925. There were no church records because Svalbard's first minister didn't arrive until 1920. There were no hospital records because the hospital was bombed during World War II.

But then she heard about some diaries written by coal miners from Longyearbyen in Svalbard. She called a coal company in Longyearbyen and asked about the diaries. Yes, they existed. No, they no longer possessed them. A local schoolteacher, the local historian, had them. Dr. Duncan called him.

"Not only did he have them," Dr. Duncan recalls, "but he was good enough to translate them for me!" The diaries recorded the deaths of seven young men who were killed by the Spanish flu. After two years of research, Dr. Duncan felt she had a chance to find her virus.

The seven men had been passengers aboard the *Forsete,* the last ship to Longyearbyen before the water froze and made sea travel impossible. Before the ship landed, flu broke out among its passengers. When it finally docked, many had to be taken to the hospital. Seven died and were buried in the local cemetery.

In 1997, Dr. Duncan made her first visit.

"I walked to the church. It's about 200 yards. And I can honestly say, it was the longest walk of my life. It's a valley. And it's completely white. And in the cemetery were about fifty white crosses. And the seven I was interested in were in the back row."

She looked down at the six crosses and one headstone and, reading the names, she began to cry. "It was overwhelming," she recalls.

Dr. Duncan began contacting the families of the dead miners and the local authorities, asking permission for her work.

"I believe a cemetery is a sacred place," she explains.

"You don't disturb cemeteries. These were young men starting out in life. I don't want people to think these are just bodies and this is cold, hard science."

The surviving family members gave their approval. Dr. Duncan quickly put together an international research team to help her. And she began asking questions. She knew that the flu virus normally stays in the body only a short time after infection. How quickly did these miners die after contracting the flu? Were they buried with the virus still in their lungs? If the miners were buried above the permafrost, they would have thawed and deteriorated. If they were buried beneath the permafrost, they would be perfectly preserved. How deeply were the miners buried? Soil that is excavated, then replaced, as in a grave, is packed together differently than soil that has not been disturbed by digging. Although it cannot "see" beneath the soil, ground-penetrating radar indicated that the ground was disturbed to a depth of at least six feet.

This was hopeful information. The bodies could be frozen, the virus preserved within their lungs. Dr. Duncan felt encouraged. The expedition moved forward.

Dr. Hilleman, the leader of the top secret 1950s expedition, was frightened. "All I can say is I hope they're not successful," he exclaimed. "I'm not so much worried about it getting into the air as about somebody catching the disease and then spreading it to other people and starting another pandemic."

Dr. Duncan promised that would not happen. The site of the digging would be covered by a tent with a special air lock, preventing any loose viruses from escaping into the surrounding countryside. All the researchers would be wearing special suits to protect them from contamination. Once the bodies were exposed, they would be kept in place and frozen. Using a drilling tool, researchers would extract very small samples from the lungs and other organs. These would be frozen at the site, placed in containers that were completely sealed, then flown back in special planes to research centers around the world.

It would all be very safe, Dr. Duncan insisted. Besides, it was necessary. To allow the flu to stay hidden was more dangerous. Though historians disagree as to how often major flu pandemics occur, Dr. Duncan believes we're due for another. "The more we learn about the 1918 flu, the better off we are."

It was all very safe. It did not, however, go as planned.

The digging began on August 4, 1998. Working within the sealed tent, five grave diggers imported from London began using spades to clear away the topsoil above the coffins of the seven miners. They planned to use jackhammers to break apart the concrete-hard permafrost. But the work proceeded quicker than expected. The diggers reached the coffins at a depth of three feet. The coffins were buried above the permafrost. This was bad news: it meant that the bodies had been repeatedly frozen and thawed for eighty years.

The scientists opened the coffins. It was immediately clear that these men had been buried in a hurry. The bodies were naked, wrapped only in newspapers. Though the scientists would not disclose what the miners looked like, many expressed disappointment. The bodies were not perfectly preserved.

But what about the radar findings? Dr. Duncan could only guess. Perhaps the original grave diggers had used dynamite to blast through the permafrost. This could have disturbed the soil to a depth of six feet and tricked the radar. The original grave diggers, hurrying to bury the diseased bodies, could have set the coffins on the pile of rubble, then covered them with dirt.

The team, dressed in their safety space suits, continued with their work. They removed more than a hundred tissue samples, some from the lungs of the miners, which were then flown to research labs around the world. It could take years to fully analyze these samples. Dr. Duncan still has hope.

A NOTE LEFT BEHIND

What if we could get the 1918 flu to tell us about itself, without risking our lives, or the lives of others? The RNA of the flu, the instructions that make the virus work, consists of about 15,000 bases, or bits of information. Could this RNA be removed from the virus and studied safely? Could the RNA of the 1918 flu be compared to the RNA of recent flus to see where and how they differ?

With the belief that what we cannot understand today, we may understand tomorrow, the Armed Forces Institute of Pathology has been collecting samples of diseased human tissue for the past 130 years.

It is the largest collection of its kind, containing more than two and a half million pieces of tissue, organs, and body parts. Most important to Dr. Jeffrey Taubenberger, the leader of a team investigating the 1918 flu, seventy of those samples are from American soldiers who died from that flu.

Could any of these samples tell us anything?

Until recently, the answer was no. When tissues are removed from a dead body, they are fixed in a chemical called formaldehyde that preserves the tissue and keeps it from decaying. Formaldehyde also kills viruses. Further damage is done to any potential virus when these tissues are embedded in wax, and placed, as Dr. Taubenberger explains, "on something like a really thin bologna slicer that makes unbelievably thin little slices, like the thickness of your hair, or even thinner. The sample is then put on a glass slide and stained with a dye so that the tissues can be looked at under the microscope."

Another factor worked against Dr. Taubenberger. The flu virus spends very little time inside the bodies of its victims. Within days it invades, is reproduced, and is then coughed or sneezed out to infect others. While the flu's damage can linger for weeks, especially if it's followed by pneumonia, the virus itself is gone. If any of these tissue samples still harbored the flu virus, they would have to come from somebody who had died quickly after infection.

In 1995, Dr. Taubenberger began examining the autopsy slides of seventy soldiers. Of these, he searched for any men that had died less than a week after they first showed symptoms of the disease. This left him with seven candidates. Within those seven, Dr. Taubenberger found his man, or at least, the slide from his man.

He was a twenty-one-year-old private from New York stationed at Fort Jackson, South Carolina, in 1918. His name was Roscoe Vaughan. He had no record of ever being seriously ill before. On September 19, he arrived at the camp hospital with the symptoms of acute pneumonia. He died six days later, at 6:30 in the morning. By noon, doctors had performed an autopsy on him, taking pieces of his body to be preserved for future study.

Dr. Taubenberger began trying to find the virus's genetic material from this slide. He used techniques he had helped to pioneer. It was long, difficult, and tedious work. Two years later, in March 1997, Dr. Taubenberger published a paper describing his initial findings. The news made the front page of the *New York Times*. Dr. Taubenberger had found some of the genetic material for the virus. For the first time, someone had read about the operating instructions for the 1918 flu.

In San Francisco, Johan Hultin, then seventy-two years old and a retired pathologist, caught a glimpse of Dr. Taubenberger's discovery in a science journal.

"I wrote him and asked him if he wanted another specimen from another part of the world," Dr. Hultin recalls. He offered to return to Alaska. He would go back to the Teller Mission, which was now called Brevig. He would dig up that same grave. Since Dr. Taubenberger didn't need the virus to be alive to get its information, Hultin would not confront the same problems he had forty-six years earlier.

Dr. Taubenberger was interested. The more specimens he had, the more information he could put together about the 1918 virus.

"When can you go?" he asked.

"I told him, I couldn't go that week, but I could go the next. I just took off," Hultin explained. Traveling by himself, he could move fast. "There's just an expedition of one, no arguments with others. I carried a duffel bag with some autopsy gear, specimen bottles, a sleeping bag, and some chemicals to preserve the tissue samples."

Arriving at Brevig, Hultin got permission to place his sleeping bag on the floor of a local school and to use the kitchen to cook his food. Eskimo authorities also granted him permission to reopen the same grave he had explored all those years ago. Four young men in the village helped him dig.

Hultin wasn't worried about exposing himself and his assistants to the flu. In 1951, he had tried everything he could to awaken the flu without luck. The virus was dead, he reasoned. There was no danger. After three days, they came upon four bodies at a depth of seven feet. While three of these bodies were mostly skeletal, the fourth, that of an obese woman, was well preserved.

Being overweight was not common among Eskimo women eighty years ago. Yet it was her extra fat that probably protected this woman's organs from decaying. Hultin took lung tissue samples from all four bodies, preserving each in his chemicals. He knew the woman's lungs would be his best bet. He was right.

Dr. Johan Hultin examines the remains of an Alaskan flu victim in 1997. *Courtesy of Dr. Johan Hultin.*

Dr. Taubenberger was able to use the Eskimo woman's tissue samples to find more genetic material of the 1918 flu. He also discovered another useful tissue sample from a soldier who had died in the pandemic.

What secrets did these samples reveal? So far, the information is not complete.

"Right now," Dr. Taubenberger says, "we have only 10 percent of the genetic information. Because it's so old, it's degraded, cut up into small pieces. What we're trying to do is put it together like a jigsaw puzzle."

The entire process will take years. But so far, his work suggests that the flu started in birds.

"It clearly had passed through pigs," Dr. Taubenberger says. "An interesting example of that was the 1976 swine flu outbreak."

Yet the 1976 outbreak killed only one person, then disappeared. Clearly, being a swine flu is not enough to explain the viciousness of the 1918 strain. Why was it so much more lethal than any other flu?

As he continues to examine more RNA, Dr. Taubenberger would like to compare the genetic information of the 1976 strain of flu with the 1918 strain. He would also like to find more samples from 1918 victims. By comparing RNA, Dr. Taubenberger hopes some odd base in the 1918 strain will draw his attention and lead to the discovery of one of the great secrets of the twentieth century.

EPILOGUE
WAITING FOR THE FLU

The world is a different place than it was in 1918. While there is still no effective cure for the flu, there are new drugs that attack viruses that could be helpful in many situations. There are antibiotics to prevent and fight the bacterial pneumonia that killed so many people after they were hit with the flu. There are vaccines. There is even a nasal spray being developed for children that will make them immune to whatever flu is circulating that year.

But there are still a few reasons to worry. First, not every country is as lucky as we are. Many poor countries do not have adequate health programs. They cannot afford to produce and distribute many of the medicines that they would need to protect their citizens.

"We don't have to have another pandemic as bad as the 1918 pandemic to be concerned," says Dr. Nancy Cox of the Centers for Disease Control. Dr. Cox is responsible for keeping an eye on flu outbreaks around the world. "Even in the 1957 pandemic, there were lots of deaths, society was disrupted, schools were shut down, and businesses were closed."

Certain conditions need to exist for a flu pandemic to arise. First, the RNA of the flu virus must change so much, its shift must be so great, that there are no people around with any immunity to it. Second, a pandemic strain of the flu must be sturdy and contagious. It must travel easily from one person to another. Third, it must reproduce well in epithelial cells. If a new flu strain arises and meets these criteria, a pandemic is possible.

It is Dr. Cox's job to help monitor flu outbreaks around the world, to help get each year's vaccine ready, and to keep an eye on any suspicious new strains of the flu. The CDC is part of the World Health Organization's global surveillance program, which connects 110 laboratories in more than eighty countries. Scientists in each of these labs study every new outbreak, ready to sound the alert if a new dangerous flu surfaces. If a new pandemic did arise, these scientists would set in motion an all-out effort to develop a vaccine for the new strain. Governments would contact vaccine manufacturers, and the vaccine manufacturers would have to rush to get their vaccine produced, tested for safety, and ready to be shipped.

What would happen in the United States with a population of more than 250 million people?

"You would need six to eight months to vaccinate the entire country," says Dr. Cox. "Maybe the first thirty or forty million doses would be ready at four months. You'd have to get the priority groups vaccinated first. These folks would be the ones who were essential to the community. We're talking about firemen and policemen and particularly health care workers. We would need them to be well so they could take care of the sick. This was a horrible problem in 1918."

After these groups are vaccinated, high-risk groups would be next. These would be the people in special danger from the flu: people with heart ailments, respiratory problems, diabetes, the very old, and any other group this new strain specifically targeted.

Police and fire departments were especially hard hit by the 1918 flu epidemic. These officers in Seattle, Washington, hoped that their masks would keep them safe. *Courtesy of the American Red Cross.*

"We're certainly in much better shape than we were in 1918," says Dr. Taubenberger. "It would still be extremely difficult, and while it may be possible to win a massive effort between private drug companies and the government to make enough vaccine quickly enough to vaccinate a large percentage of the United States, I'm sure that those resources would not be available for the world at large."

Would that mean that people in poorer countries would be in severe danger if another pandemic arose?

"Absolutely," Dr. Taubenberger says. "The vast majority of people in the developing world don't have these resources. Europe and the United States, and Australia and Canada would have these kinds of resources, but a lot of countries would not. So a virus of this nature would still be incredibly lethal."

BIBLIOGRAPHY

Alcamo, Edward. *The Microbiology Coloring Book.* New York: Harper-Collins, 1996.

Altman, Lawrence K., M.D. " 'Bird Flu' Reveals Gaps in Plans for Possible Global Outbreaks." *New York Times,* January 6, 1998.

Clendening, Logan. *Source Book of Medical History.* New York: Dover, 1942.

Crosby, Alfred, *America's Forgotten Pandemic: The Influenza of 1918.* Cambridge. Cambridge University Press, 1989.

The Defending Army. Alexandria, Virginia: Time-Life Books, 1994.

Dutton, Diana. *Worse than the Disease.* New York: Cambridge University Press, 1988.

Fettner, Ann Giudici. *The Science of Viruses.* New York: William Morrow, 1990.

Ghendon, Youri. "Introduction to Pandemic Influenza Through History." *European Journal of Epidemiology* V. August 10, 1994, pages 451–53.

Hazeltine, N. S. "Scientists Seek 1918 Flu Virus." *Washington Post,* October 11, 1951.

Heinz, Robin Marantz. *A Dancing Matrix.* New York: Vintage Books/Random House, 1993.

Kolata, Gina. "Genetic Material of Virus from 1918 Flu Is Found." *New York Times,* March 21, 1997.

————. "Lethal Virus Comes Out of Hiding." *New York Times,* February 24, 1998.

Lackman, D. B., and R. N. Philip. "Antibodies in Alaskans Relative to 1918–1919 Influenza." *American Journal of Hygiene,* Vol. 75, May 1962, pages 324–28.

McCord, Carey. "The Purple Death." *Journal of Occupational Medicine,* November 1966, pages 593–98.

Palmer, Edwina, and Geoffrey Rice. "A Japanese Physician's Response to Pandemic Influenza." *Bulletin of the History of Medicine,* Vol. 66, 1992, pages 560–77.

Patterson, David, and Gerald Pyle. "The Geography and Mortality of the 1918 Influenza Pandemic." *Bulletin of the History of Medicine,* Vol. 65, 1991, pages 4–21.

Snape, William, MD, and Edward Wolfe, Ph.D. "Influenza Pandemic: Popular Reaction in Camden, New Jersey, 1918–1919." *New Jersey Medicine,* Vol. 84, No. 3, March 1987, pages 173–76.

Springer, John. "1918 Flu Epidemic in Hartford, Connecticut." *Connecticut Medical Journal,* Vol. 55, No. 1, January 1991, pages 43–47.

Thomison, J. B. "Disease in Nashville: A Short History." *Journal of the Tennessee Medical Association,* Vol. 71, April 1978, pages 265–70.

Wilford, John Noble. "In the Norwegian Permafrost, a New Hunt for the Deadly 1918 Flu Virus." *New York Times,* August 21, 1998.

————. "Quest for Frozen Pandemic Virus Yields Mixed Results." *New York Times,* September 8, 1998.

Wright-St. Clair, R. E. "Influenza in New Zealand and the Doctors Who

Died from It." *New Zealand Medical Journal,* Vol. 96, October 1983, pages 765–68.

Zimmerman, Barry, and David Zimmerman. *Killer Germs.* Chicago: Contemporary Books, 1996.

INDEX

(Page numbers in *italic* refer to illustrations.)

Nashville, TN, flu of 1918 in, 17–20

Navy, U.S., 27–28

New Jersey Public Health Department, 50

New York City, flu of 1918 in, 20

New York Times, 68

New Zealand, flu of 1918 in, 16, 26

Norway, search for influenza virus in, 57–64

Palese, Peter, 34

Pandemics:
before 1918, 10–11
contemporary possibility of, 73
as risk of search for 1918 influenza virus, 62
theories about occurrences of, 52
use of term, 11
viral shifts and, 47, 73

Permafrost, flu victims buried in, 42, 57–64

Philadelphia, PA, flu of 1918 in, 20–21

Pigs, swine flu in, 46, 51–55, 71

Pneumonia, 18, 20, 29, 66, 72

Policemen, 21, 26, 74, *75*

Poor countries, vulnerable to pandemics, 72, 76

Portugal, flu of 1918 in, 14

Prisoners of war, 16

Project George, 56–57

Public service notices, *23*

Purple Death, 7. *See also* Flu of 1918

Red Cross Motor Corps, *21*

Red Cross voluteers, *12*

Refugees, 16

RNA (ribonucleic acid), 35
of 1918 flu virus, 65, 71
changes in, 47, 73

Russia, 39, 57

St. Louis, MO, flu of 1918 in, *21*

Samoa, flu of 1918 in, 16, 26

San Francisco, CA, flu of 1918 in, 24, 28

Sanitation workers, 21, 26

Seattle, WA, flu of 1918 in, *75*

Shifts, 47, 73

Smith, Wilson, 30–32

Sneezing, 20, 22, 34, 35, 66